AF413136

Maya for Kids

An Enthralling Guide to the Maya Civilization, Cities, and Secrets of an Ancient World

Table of Contents

INTRODUCTION

The ancient Maya thrived in the jungles and forests of Central America. They lived over a thousand years ago, but they left behind an incredible legacy (something important passed down). They built towering pyramids, cracked the secrets of the stars, and created one of the most fascinating civilizations the world has ever seen.

Even though only their ruins remain, the Maya story is very much alive. Historians study it. Their descendants still live in Central America today, keeping their traditions going. And kids like you are still discovering it for the first time!

So, who were these people? They were farmers who grew crops. They were fierce warriors who built mighty cities. They were mathematicians and scientists who made discoveries still used today. They built enormous step pyramids and temples that tourists travel from all over the world to see. And they did it all thousands of years ago.

In this book, you will explore the great Maya cities that were home to tens of thousands of people. You will find out how the Maya became such incredible stargazers and why the sky mattered so much to them. Make sure to check out the end-of-chapter activities to test your knowledge!

Are you ready for an adventure? Grab your explorer's hat because we are heading into the jungles of Central America to uncover the world of the ancient Maya!

The Maya lived in a part of the world called *Mesoamerica* (*mess-o-uh-mer-i-kuh*). This region stretches from southern Mexico into parts of Central America. It includes Guatemala, Belize, Honduras, and El Salvador.

Mesoamerica.[1]

The Maya were farmers who mostly grew corn. They were also hunters and gatherers who learned to live off the land.

Over time, they built amazing cities. Some held over 100,000 people! Their temples rose ten stories into the sky. They also built palaces, houses, and trading ports along the coast.

The Maya were more than great builders. They were thinkers and inventors too. They created their own writing system using pictures and symbols called *hieroglyphics* (*hi-row-gliff-icks*). The ancient Egyptians used something very similar on the other side of the world. Each image stood for a sound or a meaning.

The Maya were also skilled at math and *astronomy* (*as-tron-o-mee*), the study of the sun, moon, and stars. They tracked the night sky without a telescope. They used what they learned to make calendars that told them when to plant crops and when to harvest. They also made beautiful pottery and carved images into stone statues and temple walls.

Today, travelers still visit the ruins of their great cities, many of which are found hidden deep in the jungle.

Maya stela.[2]

The Land of the Maya

The Maya homeland was mostly jungle and rainforest. It was warm and humid all year long. Today, that land stretches across southern Mexico and parts of Central America. Many of the greatest Maya cities were built on the Yucatan Peninsula.

The jungle was full of wildlife. Howler monkeys swung through the trees. Iguanas sunned themselves on rocks below. Wild turkeys and **tapirs** (pig-like animals) roamed the forest floor. Rodents called *agouti* (*ah-goo-tee*) scurried about. They look like a big squirrel or guinea pig and can grow as large as a housecat. Raccoon-like animals called *coati* (*koh-wah-tee*) also called the jungle home. Colorful birds filled the trees, and sea turtles swam along the coastline.

It was in this wild, lush place that the Maya built their great civilization.

Coati.[3]

Where Did the Maya Come From?

That is a question historians are still working to answer. People lived in the Maya region as far back as 11,000 BCE. The history of the Maya is usually split into three time periods:

- Pre-Classic period — 1800 BCE to 250 CE
- Classic period — 250 CE to 900 CE
- Post-Classic period — 900 CE to the 1500s CE

Many of the earliest Maya cities were built in what is now Guatemala. Over time, the Maya spread north and south, building big cities and small towns along the way. As different groups settled in new areas, they developed different languages, beliefs, and diets, much like how cultures around the world differ today.

The Maya were expert farmers. They learned to grow crops on hillsides before many other cultures had figured out how. They adapted what they grew to fit the land around them.

Ruins of Calakmul.[4]

What Happened to the Maya?

By around 800 CE, great cities like Tikal had been abandoned. No one knows for sure why. Some historians think a long **drought** (a long period without rainfall) forced people to leave. Others think years of fighting between Maya groups took a heavy toll. Then, centuries later, Spanish invaders arrived and brought more war and change.

But the Maya did not disappear. Their descendants still live in Central America today and carry on many of their traditions. New ruins are still being found, and each discovery teaches us something new. We know that Maya society had different classes. There were rulers, nobles, peasants, and slaves. And we know the Maya shaped much of their lives around what they saw in the sky.

Kaminaljuyu ruins in Guatemala.[5]

"Many ancient Maya cities were nearly swallowed by the jungle before archaeologists found them!"

Let's test your knowledge! Fill in the blanks in the statements below.

If you get stuck, look back at the chapter. The answers are at the end of the book.

1. The study of the stars, the moon, and the planets is known as ______________.

2. The ancient Maya lived in a part of the world known as ______________.

3. Many of the great cities of the Maya have been found in the ______________.

4. The Maya used pictures and symbols called ______________ to write down their language.

5. The Maya built cities that could hold over ______________ people.

You can find clocks and calendars in nearly every home today. They tell us when to wake up, what day it is, and how much time has passed. But how did the ancient Maya keep track of time when all they had was the sun and the stars?

The answer is astronomy, the study of the stars and planets. The Maya watched the night sky carefully and used what they saw to guide almost every part of their lives. Their religious leaders believed that the stars and planets were gods. Those gods told them when to plant crops, when to harvest, when to hold religious ceremonies, and even when to go to war.

To get a better look at the sky, the Maya built special buildings called *observatories* (*ob-zerv-a-tor-eez*). These were often built on top of pyramids or high platforms.

El Caracol.[6]

One ancient observatory still stands today in *Chichen Itza* (*chee-chen eet-sah*). It is known as El *Caracol* (*kah-rah-kohl*), which means "the snail" in Spanish. It is named for the spiral staircase inside. El Caracol was built to help Maya priests track the path

of Venus. Sometimes, Venus appeared in the morning sky. Other times, it appeared in the evening. Some historians believe Maya kings might have planned their battles based on where Venus was in the sky.

The Maya did not just watch the sky. They also wrote down what they saw. They tracked the phases of the moon and the movement of the stars. Over time, they were even able to predict when eclipses would happen. They called a solar eclipse the "eating of the sun."

They recorded all of this on paper made from tree bark. These bark paper books are called *codices* (*koh-duh-seez*). Sadly, many of them were destroyed after the Spanish arrived, so only a few survive today.

Instead of letters, the Maya used symbols called hieroglyphs to write. Each glyph had its own meaning. It could be a name, an animal, or an idea. The ancient Egyptians used a very similar system.

Maya glyph of Day 10.[7]

The Tzolk'in and Haab Calendars

The Maya created two main calendars. The first was the *Tzolk'in* (*tsole-keen*), also called the Sacred Almanac or Divine Calendar. It counted 260 days and was used by priests to keep track of holy days and religious ceremonies. It is often shown as two wheels. There was a small wheel carved with thirteen numbers fitted inside a larger wheel carved with the names of twenty days. The wheels worked together like gears, ticking through each combination of number and day name.

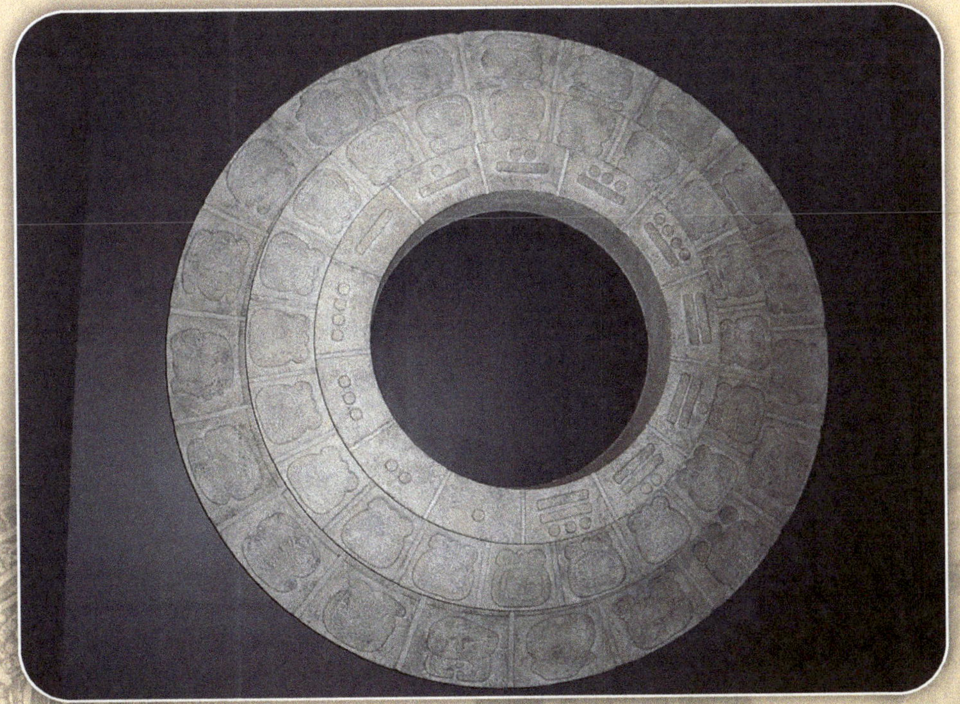

Maya Divine Calendar.[8]

The second calendar was the *Haab* (*hahb*). This was a solar calendar with 365 days, just like the calendar we use today. The Maya used it in daily life to know when to plant crops, when to hunt, and when to celebrate important dates.

Both calendars were different from ours in one interesting way. Every single day had its own glyph, linked to a specific animal, plant, god, or goddess. The Maya believed that each day, a different god carried the world from sunrise to sunset. Then, they passed it on to the next god the following day.

The Haab calendar had five days without names. These days were called Wayeb (why-eb). The Maya believed these were unlucky days when something bad was sure to happen.

When the Tzolk'in and Haab calendars were used together, they created a cycle that repeated every fifty-two years. Historians call this the Calendar Round. It was a useful way for the Maya to keep track of longer stretches of time. Fifty-two years was not always long enough. To record hundreds or even thousands of years of history, the Maya needed something bigger.

The Long Count Calendar

The Maya were also very skilled at math. They used a number system based on twenty instead of ten. They were one of the first civilizations in the world to use the number zero, something that many other ancient cultures had not figured out yet. This made it possible for them to count very large numbers and track long periods of time.

That is exactly what the Long Count calendar was built to do. While the Tzolk'in and Haab tracked days, the Long Count tracked years. The Maya counted a little over five thousand years, starting from the year 3114 BCE. It used five units of time:

- 1 day
- 20 days
- 360 days
- 7,200 days
- 144,000 days

The Maya carved Long Count dates onto tall stone pillars called *stelae* (*stee-lee*). These pillars told stories of important events in Maya history.

Like our modern calendar, the Long Count worked in cycles. When one cycle ended, a new one began. That is just like how we celebrate the end of one year and the start of another on January 1st.

For a long time, many people believed the Maya Long Count would end on December 21st, 2012, and that the Maya had predicted the end of the world. Scientists now believe it simply marked the end of one cycle and the start of a new one.

Astronomy and Religious Beliefs

For the Maya, watching the sky was about much more than keeping track of time. They believed that the positions of the stars and planets revealed what their gods wanted from them and what the future held.

One of their most important gods was the sun god *Kinich Ahau* (*kee-neech ah-hau*). The Maya believed he traveled across the sky as the sun each day. At night, he transformed into a jaguar to journey through the Maya underworld, known as *Xibalba* (*shee-bal-bah*).

Maya ceremony.[9]

For the Maya, every movement in the sky meant something. Every star, every planet, and every phase of the moon was connected to a god or goddess. Those gods shaped how the Maya lived, from when they planted their crops to when they went to war. This connection between the sky and their beliefs helped the Maya survive for thousands of years.

The ruins they left behind still show us just how closely they watched the world above them.

Decide whether the following statements are true or false.

1. The Maya believed that the stars and planets could predict future events.

2. The Haab calendar was also known as the Calendar of the Underworld.

3. The Tzolk'in calendar counted out more than five thousand years.

4. The ancient Maya made paper out of tree bark.

5. Maya kings sometimes planned their battles by watching the planet Venus.

The Maya built many large cities throughout Mesoamerica. They were not all ruled by one emperor. They were more like separate kingdoms that sometimes traded with each other and sometimes went to war.

Some cities sat along busy trade routes. Others were built in spots that were easier to defend. Many of these cities were hidden under thick jungle for hundreds of years before archaeologists (*ar-kee-ol-uh-jists*), scientists who study ancient places and people, began to uncover them. Today, their ruins give us an amazing look at how the Maya lived.

Tikal

The city of *Tikal* (*tee-kahl*) was one of the most important Maya cities. Built deep in the rainforest of what is now Guatemala, it was home to one of the mightiest kingdoms in the Maya world. Tikal sits in the heart of what is known as the Maya Forest, a region famous for its ruins and rich history.

Tikal was wealthy and had a strong military. Power was passed down from father to son, with many generations of kings, known as *dynasties* (*dye-nuh-steez*), ruling over the region.

But Tikal did not rule alone. Another powerful Maya city called Calakmul was its greatest rival. For many years, the two cities fought wars to control trade and power in the region. This helps explain why cities like Tikal needed such large armies.

More than twenty-four pyramids have been found in Tikal, along with temples, palaces, and open gathering spaces called **plazas**. Most were built from stone. The pyramids and temples were built for rulers and the upper class. Many were built over the burial chambers of kings.

Temple of the Jaguar.[10]

Two of the most famous pyramids face each other across a large plaza. The first is believed to be the tomb of a powerful king named Jasaw Chan K'awiil I. It is also known as the Temple of the Jaguar. The second pyramid, called the Temple of Masks, is believed to have been built in honor of his wife, Lady Lahan Unen Mo'.

Nearby, a group of structures called the Plaza of the Seven Temples is covered in Maya hieroglyphics. Many of these carvings date back to the Early Classic period, around 250 to 600 CE. Others are believed to be even older, carved as far back as 600 BCE.

Palenque

Another great Maya city was *Palenque* (*pah-len-kay*). It was smaller than Tikal, but it is one of the most studied Maya sites in the world. Many well-preserved ruins have been found there, allowing historians to piece together a detailed picture of life in the city.

Palace at Palenque.[11]

Like other Maya cities, Palenque blended into the forests and jungles around it. At its heart stands a pyramid called the Temple of the Inscriptions. Inside is the stone coffin, called a *sarcophagus* (*sar-koff-uh-gus*), of one of the city's greatest rulers, King Pakal the Great. Pakal ruled for nearly seventy years and lived to be about eighty years old. That was very old for people in the ancient world! The city grew wealthy under his rule, and many believed he became a powerful ancestor spirit after he died.

Temple of the Inscriptions at Palenque.[12]

The lid of Pakal's stone coffin is one of the most famous pieces of Maya art ever found. Its glyphs tell us what the ancient Maya believed about death and rebirth. They thought that dying was just part of a journey into another world.

FUN FACT

The stone lid over Pakal's coffin is about twelve feet long and seven feet wide. It weighs around seven tons. It weighs about the same as a full-grown African elephant!

Pakal's tomb cover. Some people
say it shows a seated astronaut.[13]

The tomb was discovered in 1952 at the bottom of the nine-layered pyramid. The ruins of Palenque also include a large central palace, a ball court, many temples, and a tower that might have been used as an observatory to track the stars and the moon.

Chichen Itza

One of the largest and most famous Maya cities was *Chichen Itza* (*chee-chen eet-sah*). Its name means "at the mouth of the well of the Itza." Built between 900 and 1200 CE, the city was home to as many as fifty thousand people. It stretched over two miles on each side and was located in the eastern part of the Yucatan Peninsula.

The region around Chichen Itza was full of underground rivers, caves, and limestone formations. The Maya used that limestone to build their impressive structures. The city's location near the northern coast also made it a busy trading hub. Goods arrived by canoe from all directions. **Cacao** (the plant used to make chocolate), feathers, and salt came from the Caribbean coast. Tortoise shells and fish came from the Gulf Coast. **Bark cloth** (used to make paper and clothing) and shells came from the Pacific.

The builders of Chichen Itza designed their most important structures to line up with the movements of the stars and the sun.

At the center of the city stands a great pyramid built to honor *Kukulkan* (*koo-kool-kahn*), a feathered serpent god of the Maya. The pyramid was actually built on top of an even older pyramid.

The pyramid of Kukulkan has 91 steps on each of its 4 sides. Add the platform at the top, and the total comes to 365, one for every day of the year.

During the spring and autumn equinoxes, the setting sun casts a shadow that looks like a giant serpent slithering down the side of the pyramid. Many historians believe this was carefully designed to honor Kukulkan.

Like Palenque, the ruins of Chichen Itza also include a ball court and an observatory. The Maya played a ball game in these courts using a heavy rubber ball. Players had to keep the ball in the air using only their hips, elbows, or knees.

The shadow cast on the temple during the spring equinox.[14]

Sacrifice in Maya Cities

Religion was a big part of life in every Maya city. The Maya believed that blood was a source of food for their gods. Giving blood or even being sacrificed was considered an honor. Most of the time, a living person would offer blood through a small cut. This was especially common among rulers and nobles, who felt proud to make such an offering. Blood was also given before battles or as a way of asking a god for forgiveness.

The Maya also sacrificed animals to their gods. In some cases, they sacrificed humans, though this was less common. Images of these ceremonies have been found carved into temple walls and painted on pottery and bark-paper books in cities such as Tikal, Chichen Itza, and Palenque.

A watercolor of the ruins at Chichen Itza.[15]

While religion played a big role in Maya life, there was much more to their world than temples and rituals. In the next chapter, we will take a closer look at how the Maya lived from day to day.

Imagine that you are in charge of building a Maya city. Draw your own map of what this city might look like. Do not forget to add important buildings like palaces, temples, pyramids, and markets.

Explain why you placed the buildings where you did. Did you consider water, sunlight, and defense?

The Maya lived in a society made up of different **classes**, groups of people based on wealth and power. At the top were the nobles and rulers, such as kings and their families. Religious leaders were part of this upper class too. They had the most power, lived comfortably, and wore fine clothing.

Priests were among the most powerful people in Maya society. Sometimes, they had great influence over the king himself. Everyone, from common people to kings and queens, gave priests gifts or whatever they needed. In return, priests performed religious ceremonies and spoke to the gods on behalf of the people. They lived separately from everyone else. They had servants and lived very comfortable lives.

Each Maya city had its own ruling family that controlled daily life. Power was usually passed from father to son, though sometimes a family rose to power after winning a great battle.

Nobles did not work the same way as common people. Some served as military leaders. Others made their living through trade and running businesses. Children of noble families sometimes attended special schools where they learned to read, write, and study religion.

Fun Fact

Most scribes and nobles could read and write the ancient Maya symbols carved into the many temples, palaces, and pyramids.

Below the nobles and priests were soldiers, merchants, and skilled craftspeople such as potters and weavers. These people lived simple but respectable lives.

The lowest class was made up of farmers and slaves. A person could become a slave if they were captured in war, committed a crime, or fell into debt.

In most cases, people stayed in the class they were born into. Farmers raised farmers. Builders raised builders. Even so, any man could become a soldier. Soldiers were deeply respected in Maya society.

Women played an important role too. They could farm, run businesses, take part in politics, and hold positions in government. They also cooked and raised their families.

Children were expected to help from a young age. They learned to cook, build, hunt, farm, and gather at harvest time. These were skills they would need for the rest of their lives.

The Maya made most of their clothing from cotton. Common people wore simple garments, while nobles wore colorful clothing decorated with feathers, shells, and jade jewelry.

What Did the Maya Eat?

Farming was an important part of Maya life. Corn, called maize, was the most important crop of all. The Maya used maize to make tortillas and porridge to feed their families every day. They also grew beans, squash, and chili peppers.

Cacao was another important crop. The Maya used it to make a bitter chocolate drink that was very different from the sweet chocolate we know today. This drink was considered special and was often used in ceremonies.

What Did a Maya Village Look Like?

A Maya village or city was built around a central open space called a *plaza* (*pla-za*). This was where people came together for ceremonies, celebrations, and trade.

Markets were held in the plaza. Farmers, merchants, and craftspeople came there to buy and sell food, tools, pottery, cloth, and other goods. It was a busy place. It would be a little like a farmers' market today.

The most important buildings in any Maya city were its pyramids and temples. Many had a flat top with a temple built on it. A person could reach the top by climbing steep stone steps. Priests and rulers usually climbed the pyramids to perform ceremonies in the temple at the top.

Modern model of Tikal.[16]

Nobles and wealthy families lived close to the plaza in solid stone homes. Common people lived farther from the center in simpler homes made from wooden poles covered with dried grass or vines.

A typical Maya home was just one large room. These homes did not stand for very long because they were made from wood and thatch. Heavy rains and flooding often meant repairs or rebuilding.

One clever building technique the Maya used was called a corbel arch. Instead of a rounded arch, Maya builders stacked stones so that each one jutted out a little further than the one below until the two sides met in the middle. It was an advanced method for its time and can still be seen in Maya ruins today.

> Some Maya temples were built to align with the moon, the sun, and the stars.

Traditional Maya house.[17]

Maya corbel arch.[18]

Daily Life in a Maya City

Daily life for the Maya was a mix of hard work and fun. People gathered in the plaza on market days and celebrated religious events and festivals together. One of their favorite pastimes was the famous Maya ballgame. Players used a heavy rubber ball and had to keep it in the air using only their hips, knees, or elbows. No hands allowed. Do you think you could do it?

Modern reenactment of a Maya ritual.[19]

Religion was a big part of daily life for the Maya. The gods and spirits of the Maya shaped how people lived, worked, and celebrated. Cities sometimes fought each other over land or power, which made life dangerous. But the Maya were also a people who cared deeply about their families, their traditions, and the world around them.

Choose the correct word to fill in the blanks.

1. The _______________ arch is found in many ancient Maya ruins. (Masterson/corbel)

2. Maya temples were built to align with the moon, the sun, and the ______________. (stars/trees)

3. The people lived in a society made of different _______________ (classes/castes)

4. The Maya used cacao to make a bitter _______________ drink. (chocolate/fruity)

5. Among the Maya, only nobles and _______________ could read and write the hieroglyphs. (scribes/farmers)

The ancient Maya, like many cultures around the world, had their own stories about how the world was made. Different groups of Maya often told their own versions of these stories, so the names and details could change from place to place.

The Maya believed that gods and goddesses controlled everything in the world. They made the weather. They guided the sun, the stars, and the moon. These gods sent signs to the Maya about when to plant crops, when to harvest, and when someone would be born or die.

Maya priests watched the stars and planets carefully to understand these messages. They used calendars to track important days for planting, harvesting, and religious ceremonies. The Maya showed respect to their gods by praying and offering gifts of food and blood.

Many Maya gods were shown with both human and animal features. Sometimes the same god was painted or carved with different faces or clothing. This showed that the god watched over the people from all four directions (north, south, east, and west).

The gods could be kind or harsh. Good behavior might bring a good harvest or good health. Showing disrespect could bring drought, bad weather, or ruined crops.

Fun FACT

The ancient Maya worshiped hundreds of gods and spirits.

Corn, called maize, was the most important crop for the Maya. It was also important in their religion. In some Maya creation stories, the gods made people out of maize dough. This made corn a symbol of life itself.

Ix Chel: The Moon Goddess

During the Classic period of Maya civilization, the moon goddess was known as *Ix Chel* (*eesh-chel*). She watched over the moon as it moved through the night sky each month. In ancient paintings and carvings, she is often shown as a young woman holding a rabbit or sitting on a throne. Some carvings show her with a snake wrapped around her neck as a symbol of her great power.

Goddess Ixchel.[20]

Ix Chel was also the goddess of healing, medicine, and childbirth. She could send gentle rain to water the crops or punish the people with floods and storms. Some historians think she stood for different stages of a woman's life, such as birth, growing old, and death.

Chaac: The Rain God

Chaac (*chahk*) was the god of rain, storms, thunder, and lightning. Rain was needed to grow crops, which made Chaac one of the most important gods in Maya culture. The Maya worked hard to keep him happy.

The rain god Chaac.[21]

Statues and paintings of Chaac often show him holding snakes or axes that he throws into the clouds to make rain. When he was angry, he could bring hurricanes, hailstorms, or floods that would destroy crops and leave people hungry.

Chaac also controlled four other weather spirits, each one watching over a different direction. These spirits were believed to live high in the mountains, hidden in the clouds.

The Maya held ceremonies to honor Chaac and ask for rain. Sometimes they made offerings by throwing them into deep water-filled sinkholes called *cenotes* (*seh-noh-tays*). The Maya believed that caves and cenotes were doorways to the underworld, a place called *Xibalba* (*shee-bal-bah*).

Because of this, cenotes were seen as sacred places where offerings could reach the gods. The Maya also sometimes threw jade and gold into these pools.

Kukulkan: The Feathered Serpent

One of the most important Maya gods was *Kukulkan* (*koo-kool-kahn*). He was also known as the Feathered Serpent. He was a great snake covered in colorful feathers.

The Maya believed he was a god of water, rain, and wind. They also believed he could travel between the world of the living and the world of the dead. Since snakes can live both above and below ground, the Maya saw the serpent as the perfect symbol for him.

FUN FACT

A pyramid in Chichen Itza was built to honor Kukulkan. Giant stone snake heads with open mouths can still be seen at the base of its steps today.

Kukulkan was one of the creator gods. Many Maya cities built temples in his honor.

A statue of Kukulkan.[22]

Itzamna: Lord of the Heavens

Itzamna (*eetz-ahm-nah*) was one of the greatest gods of the ancient Maya. He ruled the heavens and was known as a powerful creator god. In many paintings and carvings, he is shown dressed like a high priest. Some images show him as a creature with a crocodile body and a serpent's head.

In Maya stories, Itzamna was the husband of Ix Chel, the moon goddess. He was also connected to a special tree called the *Ceiba* (*say-bah*), which the Maya called the World Tree. The Maya believed this great tree stood at the center of the world. Its branches reached up into the sky, its trunk stood on the earth, and its roots stretched down into the underworld. It connected all three worlds together.

Itzamna, god of the universe.[23]

Maya Rituals

The Maya believed that happy gods brought good things, like sunshine, rain, a strong harvest, and victory in battle. Angry gods could bring earthquakes, drought, and hunger. To keep the gods happy, the Maya held rituals and ceremonies throughout the year.

One of the most important was the bloodletting ceremony. The Maya believed that offering blood to a god was a sign of deep honor and respect. They believed this would please the gods and keep life in balance. This ceremony was held during important events, like when a new king took the throne, when a king or queen got married, or before a big battle.

The ceremony usually took place in a temple at the top of a pyramid. Sometimes it was held in the open plaza below so that the people could watch. A sharp object was used to prick a finger, a lip, or the tongue. The blood was collected on bark paper, which was then burned along with **copal**, a sweet-smelling sap from a tree. The smoke was believed to carry the offering up to the gods.

A relief of the bloodletting ritual.[24]

Sometimes, bigger sacrifices were made. The Maya sacrificed animals and sometimes people.

Priests and shamans led these ceremonies. The priest performed the rituals and spoke on behalf of the people. The shaman was believed to speak directly to the gods and also worked as a healer. Kings often asked shamans for advice.

Together, priests and shamans connected the Maya people to their gods. They told the people when to plant and harvest. They even had a say in who a person could marry. During ceremonies, they wore colorful and sometimes scary costumes to show that they carried the voice and power of the gods.

Choose the correct answer to the following statements.

1. Itzamna was believed to have

   a. Lived in the sky and ruled the heavens

   b. Inhabited the body of a jaguar

   c. Controlled the movement of the sun and moon

2. Kukulkan is often shown with the head of a

   a. Crocodile

   b. Snake

   c. Jaguar

3. The bloodletting ritual or ceremony was often held

   a. In the jungle outside the city

   b. In a temple on top of a pyramid

   c. Inside a deep well

4. Chaac was also known as

   a. The serpent

   b. The sun god

   c. The rain god

   d. The Destroyer

People around the world love sports. They watch their favorite teams on television and in stadiums. They play soccer, baseball, basketball, and football. The ancient Maya loved to play sports too, and they had a ball game unlike anything played today.

The Maya of the Yucatán called this game *pok-ta-pok* (*pohk-tah-pohk*). In the Classic Maya period, it was known as *pitz* (*peets*). The game was played all across Mesoamerica. Both large and small cities built special courts just for it.

Ancient Maya ball game sites.[25]

FUN FACT

"Over one thousand ball courts have been discovered so far, most of them dating from the Post-Classic period."

The ball game is believed to have been played as far back as 2,000 BCE! While it was played for fun, it was usually more than just a sport. It could be used to settle arguments with a neighboring city. It was played to show honor to the gods. And sometimes, the loser was sacrificed as an offering.

The Ball Court

Ball courts were shaped like the letter "I." Some were small, but others were enormous. The ruins of these courts look nothing like a modern stadium.

Ball court at Chichen Itza.[26]

The biggest ball court found so far is the Great Ball Court at Chichen Itza. It is about 317 feet long and 98 feet wide. It is roughly the size of an American football field. Its walls stand 27 feet tall. The stone ring that players had to aim for sits 25 feet above the ground.

Other courts were much smaller. The ball court at Tikal, for example, measures just 52 feet long and 16 feet wide.

Ball court in Coba.[27]

The Great Ball Court at Chichen Itza also has a cool feature that kids and visitors love to discover. It has incredible sound. Even a small clap at one end of the court can be heard clearly at the other end. Historians believe this was no accident and that it was carefully built into the design.

Ball court ruins at Chichen Itza.[28]

Rules of the Game

Two teams played against each other. Each team had between two and six players. The exact rules changed depending on the region and time period, but a few things stayed mostly the same.

Players were not allowed to touch the ball with their hands. They could only hit it using their hips, thighs, elbows, or knees. It was a little like a mix between soccer and volleyball.

The goal was to keep the ball in the air and send it through a stone ring fixed high on the wall. This was very hard to do without using your hands. Points were given each time a team successfully hit the ball. Points were taken away if the ball hit the ground too many times or went out of bounds.

Ballgame goal at Chichen Itza.[29]

The ball was made of rubber from trees that grew in the tropical forests of Mesoamerica. The Maya learned how to make rubber by mixing tree sap with the juice of another plant. This made the ball strong and bouncy. It was small enough to hold in one hand, but it could weigh several pounds. It was heavy enough to cause a serious injury if it hit an unprotected part of the body.

To protect themselves, players wore thick leather belts around their hips, along with knee pads and arm guards. Some also wore padded clothing. This gear helped them strike the heavy ball with their hips and elbows without getting hurt. It took a lot of strength and skill to fling such a heavy ball high into the air using only those parts of the body.

The Maya playing the ball game.[30]

The Game and the Gods

The ball game was a big part of Maya religion. Some ancient carvings show captives being sacrificed at the end of a game. Other carvings show the players themselves being sacrificed. In some cases, the captain of the losing team was put to death.

Some historians think the entire losing team was sacrificed. Strangely, it seems even the captain of the winning team was sometimes sacrificed too. Why? The Maya believed the gods would feel honored to receive the blood of such a skilled and gifted player.

Historians are not sure exactly how often sacrifices took place. It is known that not every game ended in a sacrifice.

Beheading at a Maya ball game.[31]

To the Maya, blood was sacred. It was the force of life. Offering blood was one of the most important ways that the Maya showed respect to their gods.

The Maya believed death was not the end. It was part of a journey into the next world.

Modern-day Maya play pok-ta-pok.[32]

The Hero Twins

The Maya told many stories about a pair of brothers known as the Hero Twins. In one version of the story, the twins loved to play the ball game. But they made so much noise on the court that they angered the Lords of Death, who lived in Xibalba, the underworld.

The Lords of Death dragged the twins down into Xibalba, where they had to survive a series of tests. They passed through five houses of torture. They were locked in a dark house with a vampire bat named Zotz.

The twins used their brains and magic to survive. In the end, they defeated the Lords of Death in a ball game played in the underworld. The twins won and were lifted up into the sky, where they became the sun and the moon.

This story meant a lot to the Maya. It showed that the ball game was connected to life, death, and the journey into the next world. It also showed that good and clever people could overcome even the darkest forces.

The Maya believed that balance was at the heart of everything—day and night, sunshine and rain, life and death. Playing the ball game and honoring the gods with sacrifices was one way to keep that balance going.

Decide whether the following statements are true or false. Remember, the answers are at the back of the book if you get too stuck!

1. The Maya ball game was played in a court that was always the same size.

2. At the end of the ball game, a player from one of the teams was always sacrificed.

3. The Maya ball game used a ball made of heavy rubber.

4. The Maya still play the ancient ball game today.

5. The Hero Twins killed the Lords of Death on the ball court.

The Maya were known for many great achievements, but some of their most impressive were in math and science. They studied the stars, tracked the phases of the moon, and watched the movement of the planets. And they did all of this without telescopes or calculators!

The Maya Number System

The Maya created a clever system for writing numbers. They used a dot to represent the number one and a bar to represent the number five. A shell symbol stood for zero. Numbers were written by combining dots and bars. The number thirteen, for example, was written using two bars and three dots.

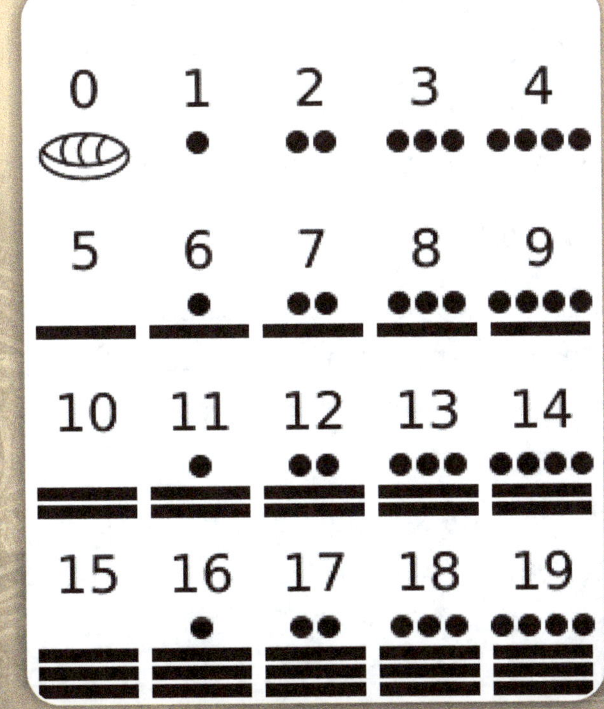

Maya number symbols.[33]

The Maya also counted differently from the way we do today. We use a base-10 system, which means we count in groups of ten. The Maya used a base-20 system, which means they counted in groups of twenty. This helped them work with very large numbers and track very long periods of time.

Maya Calendars

Using their math skills, the Maya created calendars that were remarkably accurate. In fact, they used several calendars at the same time. One tracked everyday life and the seasons. Another tracked religious ceremonies and sacred days. A third was used to count very long stretches of time.

These calendars helped the Maya know when to plant crops, when to hold ceremonies, and even when to go to war.

Watching the Sky

The Maya tracked the path of the moon every month. They studied the movement of the planets. They could even predict when a solar or lunar eclipse would happen, all using just their eyes.

One planet they paid special attention to was Venus. The Maya carefully tracked when Venus appeared in the morning or evening sky because they believed it could influence important events, such as wars. Maya kings sometimes planned battles based on the movements of Venus.

To help them study the sky, the Maya sometimes built special structures designed to line up with the sun, moon, or stars at certain times of year. One famous example is El Caracol at Chichen Itza. Historians believe this building was used as an **observatory**, a place for watching and tracking the sky.

The Maya wrote down everything they observed. They carved their findings into stone and recorded them in books made from tree bark. One of the most famous of these books is the Dresden *Codex* (*ko-dex*). It is filled with painted images and detailed math calculations about the stars and planets. Only four such bark paper books survive today. They are named after the cities where they are now kept in museums.

Dresden Codex.[35]

Maya Construction

The Maya also used math to build some of the most impressive structures of the ancient world. Their pyramids and temples still stand today, thousands of years after they were built. They were constructed without modern tools, computers, or calculators.

To build a strong pyramid, you need to understand angles, size, and balance. The Maya had a solid grasp of **geometry**, the study of shapes, angles, and measurements, long before it was taught in schools. They knew how to calculate the size of a foundation and how high they could safely build. They understood how to use corbel arches and staircases without the walls falling apart.

Maya architecture.[36]

The Maya also had a deep respect for nature. They designed their buildings to fit into the world around them. They used materials found in the jungle and shaped their structures to match the landscape.

Choose the correct word to fill in the blanks.

1. The word _______________ is the study of angles, lines, and dimensions. (algebra/geometry)

2. Maya paper was made out of _______________ (wheat fibers/tree bark fibers)

3. The Maya used a _______________ to represent the number zero. (shell/dot)

4. The Maya relied on _______________ to tell them when to plant and harvest their crops. (kings/calendars)

5. The only remaining bark paper books of the ancient Maya are named after _______________ (the Maya city where they were found/the city where they are found today)

The ancient Maya did not have grocery stores. They had to grow, hunt, or fish for everything they ate. Even without modern cooking equipment, they created flavorful meals that gave them the nutrients they needed to live and work.

Farming

Farming was hard work for the Maya. They used digging sticks and hoes made from stone blades tied to sticks. In forested areas, they had to cut down or burn trees to clear enough land to grow crops. In dry, sandy areas, they carried water from nearby rivers or streams.

Sometimes they built large storage containers called *cisterns* (*siss-turns*) to collect rainwater. In other places, they dug long canals to bring water directly to their fields.

In some areas, natural pits in the rock held water deep underground. These were called *cenotes* (*seh-no-tays*). To reach the water, the Maya built ladders from logs tied together with jungle vines. They climbed all the way down, filled pots with water, and carried them back up. It was exhausting work.

Many Maya families also grew small gardens near their homes. They planted chili peppers, tomatoes, and herbs for daily cooking.

Any farmer knows that weather makes a big difference. The Maya worried about the same things farmers worry about today, like too much rain, too little rain, or planting at the wrong time.

Maize

The most important crop the Maya grew was corn, which they called *maize* (*mayz*). Maize was the most important plant in the Maya world. The Maya believed that the gods created the first humans out of maize dough, which made corn sacred.

Maize.[37]

Maya corn was not always yellow like the corn we see today. It could be red, blue, or even several colors on the same cob. The Maya used maize to make *tortillas* (*tor-tee-yahs*) and *tamales* (*ta-mall-ays*). These foods are still popular around the world today.

Some historians believe the Maya were making tamales before they ever made tortillas.

To make tortillas, the Maya first boiled corn kernels in water mixed with wood ashes. This gave the corn a special flavor. Sometimes they boiled it with ground-up snail shells instead.

After boiling, they pounded and ground the corn into flour on a flat stone surface using a rolling tool called a *metate (meh-tah-tay)*. The flour was then mixed with chili peppers or other seasonings. This was then shaped into tortillas or bread.

Nothing went to waste. Corn husks and stalks were used for fuel or to make baskets and mats.

Stone metate.[38]

FUN FACT

The Maya often planted corn on small hills of dirt, with squash and beans growing in trenches on either side. This way, they could water three different crops at the same time. This is known as the Three Sisters technique.

Beans were another important part of the Maya diet. They were often eaten with maize. These two foods gave the body important nutrients it needed to stay healthy.

Maize.[39]

Hunting and Fishing

The Maya also hunted and fished for food. In the forests, they hunted deer, wild turkeys, rabbits, and small wild pigs called *peccaries* (*pek-uh-reez*). In some areas, they also caught iguanas and turtles. For small prey like birds and monkeys, they used slings or blowpipes loaded with clay pellets or darts. For larger animals, they used spears or a weapon called an *atlatl* (*at-laht-ul*). This tool helped them throw a spear harder and farther.

Maya living near rivers or the ocean caught fish and shellfish using spears or nets.

Atlatl and darts.[40]

Salt was also important to their diet. People living near the coast made salt by drying seawater in the sun. They traded salt with people who lived inland, where salt was hard to find.

Cacao

One of the most prized foods of the Maya was *cacao (ka-kow)*. The large pods of the cacao plant contain seeds called cacao beans. These are the same beans used to make chocolate today.

The Maya did not eat chocolate bars. Instead, they made a drink from cacao beans that was often bitter. Sometimes they mixed chili peppers or honey in it. They sometimes poured the drink from one cup to another to make it frothy. It was nothing like the sweet hot chocolate we drink today, but it was considered a special and sacred drink.

The Maya believed cacao was sacred and that the gods loved it. They offered cacao beans as gifts to their gods. Sometimes they placed bowls of cacao beans in graves to feed the dead on their journey to the afterlife. Cacao beans were also used as a form of money.

To prepare cacao, the Maya cut open the pods, pounded the seeds, and let them ferment (*fur-ment*), a process that brings out the chocolate flavor. The seeds were then dried for one or two weeks. The seeds were roasted, peeled, and ground into powder.

The Tamale

Another favorite food was the *tamal* (*ta-mall*), known today as a *tamale* (*ta-mall-ay*). Like tortillas, tamales are made from corn dough. The dough was filled with meat, vegetables, or sweet ingredients. They were wrapped in corn husks and steamed until cooked.

Maya tamal.[42]

How Did the Maya Cook?

Sometimes the Maya cooked food in large pots over a fire, much like making a stew or soup today. Other times, they used an underground pit oven. To make one, they dug a pit in the earth, lined it with wood, and placed large stones on top. After lighting the fire, the stones soaked up the heat. Once the wood had burned away and the stones were hot, food was wrapped in banana leaves and placed on the stones to cook slowly. The leaves added moisture and a flavor to the food. This type of underground oven is still used in parts of Mexico and is called a *pib* (*pib*).

Feasts

Food was an important part of Maya ceremonies and social life. Feasts were held to celebrate a good harvest or a victory in battle. At these gatherings, food was served to priests and royalty first. Then, it was shared among the people on decorated plates and bowls.

Maya plate with fish.[43]

Cacao drinks and other special foods were used in healing and religious rituals. The Maya honored the land that fed them and gave thanks to their gods through the food they grew, hunted, and prepared.

Fill in the blanks in the statements below.

1. The Maya used foods and drinks in both raw and cooked form to give as gifts to their ________________.

2. Cacao pods or beans were sometimes used as a form of ________________ by the ancient Maya.

3. Feasts were often held to celebrate a good ________________ or a successful battle or war.

4. Sometimes they dug large wells or found natural underground pools of water known as ________________ that would hold rainwater.

5. For hunting large prey, they used spears or an ________________.

At the height of their power, the ancient Maya built some of the greatest cities in the world. Millions of Maya lived across Mesoamerica. Their pyramids touched the sky. Their knowledge of math and astronomy was extraordinary. So what happened to them?

The truth is that no one knows for sure. The decline of the Maya is one of the greatest mysteries in history. Historians have some important clues.

The Collapse of the Great Cities

By around 800 to 900 CE, many of the greatest Maya cities had been abandoned. Tikal had once been home to tens of thousands of people, but it was now empty. Palenque fell silent. Other great cities across the region were swallowed up by the jungle. Historians call this the Maya Collapse.

Why did it happen? Most historians believe several things went wrong at the same time.

A photo of Tikal in 1882. The jungle growth around the city had just been removed.[44]

One major theory is drought. Scientists have found evidence that the Maya region experienced long periods without rain during this time. Without enough water, crops would have failed. People would have gone hungry. Without food, the cities could not survive.

> Scientists studied the rings inside ancient trees to find evidence of the droughts that might have caused the Maya Collapse. Tree rings can tell us a lot about the weather from thousands of years ago!

Another theory is warfare. The Maya cities often fought each other for land and power. As we learned earlier, cities like Tikal and Calakmul were rivals. Constant warfare would have weakened cities and destroyed farmland. This would have made life very hard for people.

Some historians also believe that the Maya might have damaged the environment. As their cities grew larger, they needed more and more farmland. Cutting down forests and over-farming the land might have made it harder to grow enough food over time.

Most historians today believe it was a combination of all these things that caused the great cities to fall.

The Spanish Arrive

The fall of the great cities did not mean the Maya disappeared. New cities were built in the north, including Chichen Itza and Mayapan. The Maya civilization continued for hundreds of years after the Maya Collapse.

Then, in the 1500s, Spanish explorers and soldiers arrived in Mesoamerica. They were looking for gold and land.

Led by men like Francisco de Montejo, the Spanish fought a long and brutal war against the Maya. It took the Spanish nearly 170 years to fully conquer the Maya region.

The Spanish also brought diseases like smallpox. The Maya had never encountered these diseases before. Because the Maya had no **immunity** (protection) to these diseases, a lot of people died. Some historians believe that disease killed more Maya than wars did.

The Spanish tried to erase Maya culture. They destroyed Maya books and banned religious ceremonies. They forced the Maya to convert to Christianity. A Spanish bishop named Diego de Landa ordered the burning of Maya codices. Centuries of knowledge and history went up in flames.

The Maya Today

Despite everything they faced, the Maya never disappeared. Today, millions of people in Mexico, Guatemala, Belize, Honduras, and El Salvador are descendants of the ancient

Maya. Many still speak Mayan. Some communities still use versions of the ancient Maya calendar. Traditional foods, clothing, and ceremonies continue to be passed down.

The ancient ruins of their cities continue to be studied by archaeologists. New discoveries are made every year. In fact, modern technology like laser scanning has helped researchers find entire cities hidden under the jungle that no one knew existed.

The story of the Maya is not a story of a lost civilization. It is a story of a people who built something extraordinary. They faced tremendous challenges and survived. Their descendants are still here today, carrying on a culture that stretches back thousands of years.

The temple of Tulum.[45]

Write a short story on a piece of paper about something that you learned in this book. Your story can be an adventure, such as the one about the Hero Twins. Perhaps it could be something about watching the stars or a story about what you would make for dinner tonight using only things, plants, or animals in the jungle. Have fun with your story. Let your imagination run wild!

Chapter 1

1. Astronomy
2. Mesoamerica
3. Yucatan Peninsula
4. Hieroglyphics
5. 100,000

Chapter 2

1. True
2. False
3. False
4. True
5. True

Chapter 4

1. Corbel
2. Stars
3. Classes
4. Chocolate
5. Scribes

Chapter 5

1. a. Lived in the sky and ruled the heavens
2. b. Snake
3. b. In a temple on top of a pyramid
4. c. The rain god

Chapter 6

1. False
2. False
3. True
4. True
5. False

Chapter 7

1. Geometry
2. Tree bark fibers
3. Shell
4. Calendars
5. The city where they are found today

Chapter 8

1. Gods
2. Money
3. Harvest
4. Cisterns
5. Atlatl

References

Canamayté: Maya Architecture and Sacred Geometry. "Canamayté: Maya Architecture and Sacred Geometry." *Lavaca Independiente*. lavacaindependiente.com/en/canamayte-maya-architecture-and-sacred-geometry.

"Chichen Itza." *Encyclopedia Britannica*. https://www.britannica.com/place/Chichen-Itza.

Coulter, Laurie. *Secrets in Stone: All about Maya Hieroglyphs*. Boston: Little, Brown, 2001.

Crosher, Judith. *Technology in the Time of the Maya*. Austin, TX: Raintree Steck-Vaughn Publishers, 1998.

"Eating the Sun — Eclipses and the Maya." *University of Texas at Austin News*. https://news.utexas.edu/2024/03/26/eating-the-sun-eclipses-and-the-maya/.

"Iconic Cuisine: Tamales of the Maya." *HistoricalMX*. historicalmx.org/items/show/154.

"Ixchel." *Encyclopedia Britannica*. britannica.com/topic/Ixchel.

Karasik, Carol. *Maya Gods & Monsters: Supernatural Stories from the Underworld and Beyond*. Loveland, CO: Thrums Books, 2016.

"Kukulkan." *World History Encyclopedia*. worldhistory.org/Kukulcan/.

"Living Maya Time." *Smithsonian National Museum of the American Indian*. maya.nmai.si.edu/calendar/calendar-system.

"Living Maya Time." *Smithsonian National Museum of the American Indian*. maya.nmai.si.edu/maya-sun/maya-math-game.

"Maya Architecture." *World History Encyclopedia*. worldhistory.org/Maya_Architecture.

"Maya Bloodletting Rituals." *M-Institute*. m-institute.org/MayanRituals/mayan-bloodletting-rituals.

"Maya Corn." *Trama Textiles*. tramatextiles.org/blogs/trama-blog/maize-the-epicenter-of-maya-culture.

"Maya Priests." *MrDonn.org*. mayas.mrdonn.org/priests.html.

Pipe, Jim. *Mysteries of the Mayan Calendar*. New York: Crabtree Publishing Company, 2013.

"Secrets of the Maya: Deciphering Tikal." *Smithsonian Magazine*. smithsonianmag.com/history/secrets-of-the-maya-deciphering-tikal-2289808.

"The Maya Calendar System." *Smithsonian National Museum of the American Indian*. maya.nmai.si.edu/sites/default/files/resources/The%20Maya%20Calendar%20System.pdf.

"The Maya Codices." *Archaeology Magazine*. archaeology.org/issues/november-december-2012/collection/groiler-dresden-codex.

"The Mysteries of the Maya." Chicago: World Book / Scott Fetzer Company, 2014.

"The Stargazers." *Science*. science.org/content/article/what-did-ancient-maya-see-in-stars-their-descendants-team-with-scientists-find-out.

"The Wonders of the Sarcophagus of Pakal." *ThoughtCo*. thoughtco.com/the-sarcophagus-of-pakal-2136165.

"Who Were the Maya? Decoding the Ancient Civilization's Secrets." *National Geographic*. nationalgeographic.com/history/article/who-were-the-maya.

Thompson, J. Eric S. *Maya History and Religion*. Norman: University of Oklahoma Press, 1970.

"Tikal." *Encyclopedia Britannica*. britannica.com/place/Tikal.

"Tikal National Park." *UNESCO World Heritage Centre*. whc.unesco.org/en/list/64/.

"Tikal National Park." *Latin American Studies*. latinamericanstudies.org/tikal-plaza-siete-templos.htm.

Webster, David. *The Fall of the Ancient Maya: Solving the Mystery of the Maya Collapse*. London: Thames & Hudson, 2002.

Sources for Kids

We hope you want to learn more about the Maya! Here are some great sources to explore:

Books:

Captivating History. *Maya History for Kids: A Captivating Guide to the Maya Civilization, from the Olmecs through the Founding of Teotihuacan in Ancient Mesoamerica to the Spanish Conquest.*

Conklin, Wendy. *Mayas, Incas, and Aztecs: World Cultures Through Time.*

DK. *DKfindout! Maya, Incas, and Aztecs.*

Websites:

Britannica.com—https://kids.britannica.com/kids/article/Maya/353445

History for Kids— https://historyforkids.org/ancient-mayans-facts-for-kids/

National Geographic for Kids— https://www.natgeokids.com/ie/teacher-category/aztecs-maya-inca/

Image Sources

[1] No machine-readable author provided. GringoInChile assumed (based on copyright claims), CC BY-SA 3.0 <http://creativecommons.org/licenses/by-sa/3.0/>, via Wikimedia Commons; https://commons.wikimedia.org/wiki/File:Mesoamerica_english.PNG

[2] https://commons.wikimedia.org/wiki/File:CPN_ST_B_01.jpg

[3] https://commons.wikimedia.org/wiki/File:MexicanCoati.jpg

[4] User:PhilippN, CC BY-SA 3.0 <http://creativecommons.org/licenses/by-sa/3.0/>, via Wikimedia Commons; https://commons.wikimedia.org/wiki/File:Calakmul_-_Structure_I.jpg

[5] Simon Burchell, CC BY-SA 3.0 <https://creativecommons.org/licenses/by-sa/3.0>, via Wikimedia Commons; https://commons.wikimedia.org/wiki/File:Kaminaljuyu_7.jpg

[6] Daniel Schwen, CC BY-SA 4.0 <https://creativecommons.org/licenses/by-sa/4.0>, via Wikimedia Commons; https://commons.wikimedia.org/wiki/File:Chichen_Itza_4.jpg

[7] CJLL Wright, CC BY-SA 3.0 <http://creativecommons.org/licenses/by-sa/3.0/>, via Wikimedia Commons; https://commons.wikimedia.org/wiki/File:MAYA-g-log-cal-D10-Ok.png

[8] Matthew G. Bisanz, CC BY-SA 3.0 <https://creativecommons.org/licenses/by-sa/3.0>, via Wikimedia Commons; https://commons.wikimedia.org/wiki/File:Maya_Calendar_by_Matthew_Bisanz.JPG

[9] https://commons.wikimedia.org/wiki/File:01-maya-lidar-mapping.jpg

[10] Raymond Ostertag, CC BY-SA 2.5 <https://creativecommons.org/licenses/by-sa/2.5>, via Wikimedia Commons; https://commons.wikimedia.org/wiki/File:Tikal_Temple1_2006_08_11.JPG

[11] Ricraider, CC BY-SA 3.0 <https://creativecommons.org/licenses/by-sa/3.0>, via Wikimedia Commons; https://commons.wikimedia.org/wiki/File:Palace_at_Palenque.jpg

[12] Lousanroj, CC BY-SA 3.0 <https://creativecommons.org/licenses/by-sa/3.0>, via Wikimedia Commons; https://commons.wikimedia.org/wiki/File:Tumba_de_pakal,_Chiapas.JPG

[13] User:Madman2001, CC BY-SA 2.0 <https://creativecommons.org/licenses/by-sa/2.0>, via Wikimedia Commons; https://commons.wikimedia.org/wiki/File:Pacal_the_Great_tomb_lid.svg

[14] https://commons.wikimedia.org/wiki/File:ChichenItzaEquinox.jpg

[15] https://commons.wikimedia.org/wiki/File:Adela_Breton_-_Ruins_at_Chichen_Itza_Yucatan_Mexico_Depicts_east_facade_of_Monjas_-_(MeisterDrucke-1020179).jpg

[16] https://commons.wikimedia.org/wiki/File:Tikal-Reconstruction4.jpg

[17] Belizemayawarrior, CC BY-SA 4.0 <https://creativecommons.org/licenses/by-sa/4.0>, via Wikimedia Commons; https://commons.wikimedia.org/wiki/File:San_Pablo_Traditional_Maya_house.jpg

[18] Bernard DUPONT, CC BY-SA 2.0 <https://creativecommons.org/licenses/by-sa/2.0>, via Wikimedia Commons; https://commons.wikimedia.org/wiki/File:Corbel_Arch_passage_way_-_Cob%C3%A1_Maya_site_QR_2020.jpg

[19] Juan Pablo Ramírez, CC BY-SA 4.0 <https://creativecommons.org/licenses/by-sa/4.0>, via Wikimedia Commons; https://commons.wikimedia.org/wiki/File:Mayan_Ritual.jpg

[20] https://commons.wikimedia.org/wiki/File:Goddess_O_Ixchel.jpg

[21] https://commons.wikimedia.org/wiki/File:MyanRainGodChac0180Rot.jpg

[22] Frank Kovalchek, CC BY 2.0 <https://creativecommons.org/licenses/by/2.0>, via Wikimedia Commons; https://commons.wikimedia.org/wiki/File:Serpent_head_at_the_base_of_El_Castillo.jpg

[23] https://commons.wikimedia.org/wiki/File:God_D_Itzamna.jpg

[24] British Museum, CC BY-SA 3.0 <https://creativecommons.org/licenses/by-sa/3.0>, via Wikimedia Commons; https://commons.wikimedia.org/wiki/File:Yaxchilan_lintel_15_detail.jpg

[25] No machine-readable author provided. Madman2001 assumed (based on copyright claims)., CC BY-SA 3.0 <https://creativecommons.org/licenses/by-sa/3.0>, via Wikimedia Commons; https://commons.wikimedia.org/wiki/File:Early_Mesoamerican_Ballgame_sites_1.svg

[26] Brian Snelson, CC BY 2.0 <https://creativecommons.org/licenses/by/2.0>, via Wikimedia Commons; https://commons.wikimedia.org/wiki/File:GreatBallCourt-interior.jpg

[27] https://commons.wikimedia.org/wiki/File:Coba_Ballcourt-27527.jpg

[28] Jan Zatko, CC BY-SA 3.0 <http://creativecommons.org/licenses/by-sa/3.0/>, via Wikimedia Commons; https://commons.wikimedia.org/wiki/File:Chich%C3%A9n_Itz%C3%A1_-_Juego_de_Pelota.jpg

[29] Kåre Thor Olsen, CC BY-SA 2.5 <https://creativecommons.org/licenses/by-sa/2.5>, via Wikimedia Commons; https://commons.wikimedia.org/wiki/File:Chich%C3%A9n_Itz%C3%A1_Goal.jpg

[30] Gumr51, CC BY-SA 3.0 <https://creativecommons.org/licenses/by-sa/3.0>, via Wikimedia Commons; https://commons.wikimedia.org/wiki/File:Libro_Los_Viejos_Abuelos_Foto_65.png

[31] AlejandroLinaresGarcia, CC BY-SA 4.0 <https://creativecommons.org/licenses/by-sa/4.0>, via Wikimedia Commons; https://commons.wikimedia.org/wiki/File:BeheadingPanelSBCTajin.JPG

[32] de:User:Sputnik, CC BY-SA 2.5 <https://creativecommons.org/licenses/by-sa/2.5>, via Wikimedia Commons; https://commons.wikimedia.org/wiki/File:Pok_ta_pok_ballgame_maya_indians_mexico_3.JPG

[33] Original: Neuromancer2K4 Vector: Bryan Derksen, CC BY-SA 3.0 <http://creativecommons.org/licenses/by-sa/3.0/>, via Wikimedia Commons; https://commons.wikimedia.org/wiki/File:Maya.svg

[34] https://commons.wikimedia.org/wiki/File:Maya_add.png

[35] https://commons.wikimedia.org/wiki/File:Dresden_Codex_p09.jpg

[36] User: (WT-shared) Hermann Luyken at wts wikivoyage, CC BY-SA 3.0 <https://creativecommons.org/licenses/by-sa/3.0>, via Wikimedia Commons; https://commons.wikimedia.org/wiki/File:2002.12.29_12_Sayil_Yucat%C3%A1n_M%C3%A9xico.jpg

[37] https://commons.wikimedia.org/w/index.php?curid=183925

[38] Leoboudv, CC BY-SA 3.0 <https://creativecommons.org/licenses/by-sa/3.0>, via Wikimedia Commons; https://commons.wikimedia.org/wiki/File:Tool_(metate)-UBC_2010.jpg

[39] Juan Carlos Fonseca Mata, CC BY-SA 4.0 <https://creativecommons.org/licenses/by-sa/4.0>, via Wikimedia Commons; https://commons.wikimedia.org/wiki/File:Museo_Nacional_de_Antropolog%C3%ADa_-_MA%C3%8DZ.jpg

[40] vastateparksstaff, CC BY 2.0 <https://creativecommons.org/licenses/by/2.0>, via Wikimedia Commons; https://commons.wikimedia.org/wiki/File:HL_-_Tools_of_the_Trade_(26920774763).jpg

[41] https://commons.wikimedia.org/wiki/File:Cocoa_Pods.JPG

[42] AraVazquez, CC BY-SA 4.0 <https://creativecommons.org/licenses/by-sa/4.0>, via Wikimedia Commons; https://commons.wikimedia.org/wiki/File:Tamal_colado._Mayan_food.jpg

[43] Gary Todd, CC0, via Wikimedia Commons; https://commons.wikimedia.org/wiki/File:Maya_Plate_with_Fish_Motif.jpg

[44] https://commons.wikimedia.org/wiki/File:Tikal1882.jpeg

[45] Popo le Chien, CC BY-SA 3.0 <https://creativecommons.org/licenses/by-sa/3.0>, via Wikimedia Commons, https://commons.wikimedia.org/wiki/File:Tulum_2.jpg